UNDIVIDED
RESTORING
UNITY
IN THE
CHURCH

BY
EDDIE
TURNER

DAY OF
REDEMPTION
MINISTRY

MANY WILL FALL AWAY AND BETRAY ONE ANOTHER
AND HATE ONE ANOTHER

BUT THE ONE WHO ENDURES TO THE END WILL BE SAVED

MATTHEW 24:10, 13

CONTENTS

CHAPTER ONE

DIVISION

People hate Christians. I mean, they REALLY hate us. Not everyone does, of course. But the haters are out there. In American cinema alone, Christians are portrayed as evil, judgmental, hypocritical, money-grubbing, televangelizing, demon-exorcising, phony faith-healing, homophobic, snake-handling hillbillies whose children hang out in abandoned warehouses to drink, smoke, and do crazy dances to Kenny Loggins' music. I tell ya, people have us pegged! Well, they *think* they do anyway. So, why all the hatred? There are many reasons, actually. By and large, however, it's because our behavior on the outside doesn't always match what we claim is on the inside. If you've ever seen black smoke pouring from a car sporting a bumper sticker that reads, "Protect the Environment," you know what I'm talking about.

Here's another example. Have you ever met someone who falsely claimed to be a doctor? I haven't either. People just don't do this because of how easy it can be to spot a phony. Within minutes, a Google search or some clever questioning can expose this lie. Should we have this encounter, we may not call their bluff to their face, but we'd surely leave their presence knowing there's no way that person is a doctor. We'd also be eager to share a laugh about it.

Ok, new question. Have you ever met someone whose claim to be a Christian you seriously doubted? I sure have—more times than I can count, probably. The difference between these two examples is that, while both are engaged in misinformation, one is aware they are lying, and the other believes they are telling the truth. Our reactions to each will differ as well. One is a rare spectacle worth pointing out, and the other is a ho-hum common occurrence that simply isn't worth mentioning.

While this example best describes interactions between believers and nonbelievers, our relationships with tried-and-true Christians have been veering steadily into this territory. Why is this happening? It's happening because we have failed miserably at being a church. If you were to compare two random congregations, the likelihood of them being perfectly aligned would be slim to none. As long as this remains a reality, meeting the criteria outlined in this verse from Philippians just isn't possible.

Therefore if there is any encouragement in Christ, if there is any consolation of love, if there is any fellowship of the Spirit, if any affection and compassion, make my joy complete by being of the same mind, maintaining the same love, united in spirit, intent on one purpose.

PHILIPPIANS 2:1-2

There are millions of individual churches across the globe, and none of them look exactly alike. Some are enormous and occupy acres of land, while others are rather quaint and may be difficult to spot without driving right past them. And still, some churches may not utilize buildings at all. So, while it's expected that physical churches will be drastically different from one another, their congregations were never to be unique—not when it comes to matters of the heart.

Just as worldly influences are too many to count, there are countless varieties of congregations. And many of them are divided according to how the world has skewed their image of God. Some factors that set them apart may seem rather trivial, such as acceptable attire during worship services. Proper dress, however, can be regarded as a standard of worship that other congregations whose members wear shorts and sneakers just aren't meeting. More extreme factors include blatant deviations from Scripture and corporate rituals as requirements for one's salvation. Congregations like these may believe that only its members may be saved.

When we consider all the factors that fall between these trivial and extreme examples, we see multitudes of different churches with as many divisions among their congregations. I'm sure there's a book out there dedicated to exposing the many church cultures in our world. As for *this* book, my focus will be on our individual relationships within the church and how the same worldly influences can cause divisions between us. While it's perfectly normal to have an opinion of the things happening in the world around us, the *strengths* of our opinions often produce more discord than harmony.

In the end time there will be scoffers living according to their own ungodly desires. These people create divisions and are worldly, not having the Spirit.

JUDE 1:18-19

The idea that we are in the midst of the end times can be a bit scary. At this, many have incorporated scare tactics in their approach to sharing the gospel. Despite not having any actual stats to serve as proof, I can say with certainty that no one has ever been scared into a loving relationship with God. As Jesus points out on multiple occasions in the Bible, at the time of the end, there will indeed be many who call themselves Christian and who scramble hastily to become active in church at the last minute. Should Jesus give us a week's notice, you can bet there would be a massive spike in new binge-reading Bible study groups all over the world whose members ignored his first three notices. This behavior merely exposes Jesus as a low priority—the very *lowest* priority, in fact.

If there's one thing I've learned about us humans, it's that we don't procrastinate our hearts' desires. The things we want get our full attention. And we go after them! We'll rearrange our schedules, create budgets, and even spend time reading about these things. Our friends will certainly hear about them too. We simply aren't wired to remain silent about the targets of our excitement. If you pictured a new iPad, a new car, or a new closet renovation in this example, try inserting Jesus instead. What great lengths are you going in your life to become closer to him? I'm sure you noticed the present-tense verb in that question. I added it because salvation is not a one-and-done experience.

Do you recall listening to a new song that you figured to be among your very favorites? Did you never make an effort to hear it again? Of course not. You'll listen to it and enjoy it for the rest of your life. Should the world lose power and be transformed into the stone age, you'll be singing that song out loud if you hadn't been already. While this scenario resembles our salvation, the effort put into it is God's. He decides the who, what, when, and where. None of us possess a heart for God that He didn't give to us. At this, we may conclude that those who wait until the last minute to seek God will be motived by fear of missing the boat rather than Jesus.

God uses us to accomplish his work on earth. Striving to be useful to Him is what we're all called to do. But we must proceed knowing that we are just as expendable as we are helpful in terms of our effectiveness. God *uses* us, but He doesn't *rely* on us for anything. Even on our best days, our praises to Him are marred by our selfish and unforgiving hearts. So it goes without saying that our names didn't wind up in the book of life because God knew the choices we would make. They are written because of the choice *God* made. Of the many topics we'll discuss together, this is one that we absolutely cannot afford to be divided over. Not even a little.

The God who made the world and everything in it, being Lord of heaven and earth, does not live in temples made by man, nor is he served by human hands, as though he needed anything, since he himself gives to all mankind life and breath and everything.

ACTS 17:24-25

As for why I chose to tackle subject matter that stands to get people all riled up, I can honestly say that this undertaking was not a decision I made. Just as the Holy Spirit led me away from writing my second book first, He showed me that there was a need for this teaching above what I had initially planned to write about. As much as I like to keep my material lighthearted and fun to read, it's a bit heartbreaking to see how this topic hits so close to home. And I feel it will for you as well. Even so, I'll try not to be a total downer. After all, there is indeed a bright side to all of this. And his name is Jesus.

As we begin this journey together, I pray that we will allow God's Spirit to speak to us and expose the elements in our lives that we've allowed to keep us from loving one another. As we go along, if at any time you feel I'm moving too fast, let me know and I'll try and add some extra space between the words. Whatever I can do to help. Lastly, I must confess that, as of now, this is the only chapter I've written. Don't worry, though. I'm sure I will have completed the others by the time you begin each one.

CHAPTER TWO

CONVICTION

In the previous chapter, we looked at how our character can become tarnished when we make claims about ourselves that our actions clearly refute. Not only can this behavior impact the way we see each other as believers, but also how nonbelievers see God. But what if the conflict we detect between one's words and actions is only in our minds? What if there's no actual moral clash going on? More often than you might think, there is no clash. No, we're not delusional. We may simply have misperceived the presence of conflict. This can occur during conversations with people whose feelings toward a topic are not as strong as ours. These feelings we have are called *convictions*. And not all of us, Christians included, share the same ones. When we fail to recognize this, we begin to perceive others with different convictions as hypocrites.

Much like knowledge and wisdom, morals and convictions go hand in hand despite having different meanings. Unlike morals, convictions aren't always tied to things we feel are just or unjust. Instead, we only need to believe something is real or true to have a conviction about it. Convictions represent *how* we understand truth. They are unique feelings that drive our behavior. Morals, on the other hand, are tied to what we believe is right or wrong. So, you can have morals, and you can have convictions. You can even have *moral convictions*. Mind blown, I know. Let's look at how these work.

Let's say there's a section of road that you believe is dangerous to drive on. Being extra careful while traveling it is a reaction to the conviction you have about that road. Someone with a stronger conviction might avoid that road altogether. Biblical convictions play out the same way. In the first of his two books in the Bible, Peter instructs each of us to be "sober-minded." And in John's third epistle, we are informed that being of "good health" is good for the soul. Regarding a sober mind, one person may feel this can be achieved by abstaining from watching movies or listening to music with inappropriate content. And yet another may resort to meditation in order to reach a level of mental clarity that compliments Peter's instruction. Also, for some, an effort toward being of good health may include a vegetarian diet, while others might simply bypass the ice cream section while shopping for groceries.

Being healthy and sober minded are both great things to strive for. But not everyone is expected to have convictions about them. Being physically fit, for example, may be a person's life-long goal. This same person's neighbor, however, may never darken the doorway of a gym due to feeling that he or she isn't really lacking in the fitness department. Do you remember that old saying, what's good for the goose is good for the gander? This idea doesn't really apply here. But that hasn't stopped many of us from insisting that it does. Here's an argument that might erupt between these two neighbors today.

"I don't understand why you don't want to take care of your body? That's just pure laziness!"

"Oh, I take care of it. I just don't have to put mine through hell in order to feel good about myself."

Ouch! Now let's look at God's argument against this very behavior over conflicting convictions.

One person believes he may eat anything, while the weak person eats only vegetables. Let not the one who eats despise the one who abstains, and let not the one who abstains pass judgment on the one who eats, for God has welcomed him. Who are you to pass judgment on the servant of another?

ROMANS 14:2-4

If there were charts for each sin that reflected all of our convictions, they would look like the readings of a seismograph recorded during an earthquake. The valleys and peaks of the lines would be all over the place. Regarding the many sinful behaviors that the Bible defines for us, God's regard for each for them is even across the board. To Him, they are all equally bad. You and I, however, tend to categorize sin according to how convicted we feel toward each one. We'll hardly become rattled over gossip and regard infidelity within a marriage as a more serious matter. As our convictions toward sin intensify, our ill regard for those who commit them escalates as well. This makes it tough for us to behave according to this next verse from Titus.

Remind them to be submissive to rulers and authorities, to be obedient, to be ready for every good work, to speak evil of no one, to avoid quarreling, to be gentle, and to show perfect courtesy toward all people.

TITUS 3:1-2

So, how can we show perfect courtesy toward people whose views we strenuously oppose? First and foremost, we must be able to determine the differences between *disputable* matters and *absolutes* according to Scripture. Unlike disputable matters, which involve things we can either do or not do, an absolute is something that *must* be accomplished—no matter what.

Absolutes may involve action or avoidance. For example, when Jesus commanded us to love our neighbors, he did not add clauses or exceptions. According to his teaching, we can do this in a variety of ways. But our obedience is not optional. Whatever it takes to get there, we absolutely must love one another. This includes acting lovingly toward people whose convictions do not match our own and whose sins absolutely turn our stomachs. Even our worst enemies deserve to experience the lovingkindness of our Savior.

If your enemy is hungry, give him bread to eat, and if he is thirsty, give him water to drink.

PROVERBS 25:21

While there's much more that can be said about our convictions, I don't want to downplay the importance of analyzing the actual arguments we have with each other. I also want to finally make use of the detective badge my parents gave me for Christmas when I was a kid. Aside from placing my brothers under arrest, I never really did anything with it. That ends here! In the chapters ahead, I'll test my sleuthing abilities and investigate some of the sensitive topics that divide us as Americans and as followers of Christ in an effort to expose the nature of our convictions. Are they real, or are they based on what others would have us to believe? We'll also examine how we as a church have allowed these issues to impede our directive to love one another. Ready to get started? Great. By the way, is it weird that I got a detective badge for Christmas? I never really thought about it. We can talk later.

CHAPTER THREE

POLITICS

Having taught Sunday school for twenty years, Jack treasured the relationships he made with those who joined him to study God's Word each week. Some had been a part of his class from the beginning; others' attendance ranged from 8 to 14 years. Only one couple had been coming for less than a year. Old friends and new, they were all like family to Jack. And there was nothing he wouldn't do for them, nor they for him. Because leadership roles typically call for intervention, Jack fully expected to smooth out the occasional mild disagreement among the members of his class. And he did this gracefully as needed. Still, nothing could have prepared him for the scope of the friction that was coming.

One Sunday, during the fellowship time before Jack's lesson, a political discussion began to brew within the class. Seeing that the back and forth was relevant to the previous week's topic, Jack allowed their interaction to replace the lesson he had planned. He'd done this before a time or two and found it productive and even fun. As the discussion became heated, however, Jack's confidence in his ability to restore order began to slip away. In less than ten minutes, the warm and welcoming environment had given way to hostility over opposing political views.

Some argued loudly while others who remained silent looked petrified. What disturbed Jack the most were the proverbial lines in the sand between morality and immorality that those who were vocal had drawn and presented so insistently. Despite each having the ultimate authority over right and wrong in their possession, none of their lines matched.

While Jack was able to calm the storm inside the classroom that day, those in its wake clung tightly to their frustrations. As a result, the class shrunk to half its size. Of the members who stopped coming, only two responded to Jack's prayerful invitations to return. As for the newest couple, this incident caused them to leave the church entirely. Though Jack continued to lead the class, he remained devastated as he struggled to understand how people who had been so loving toward one another for so long could allow something like politics to come between them.

In my quest to define the term *politics*, I quickly realized that doing so would be no easy task. Every online resource I encountered seemed to have a different definition; some with descriptives that I'd never associated with politics. So, I decided to craft a definition myself, which is what everyone seemed to be doing anyway. Instead of my own words, however, I chose to use only the ones that appeared within the 15 or so definitions I found online. Believe it or not, this was actually quite fun! Yes, I'm a nerd.

POLITICS

the influence of ideals over the management
of governing authorities and societal affairs

Tadaaa! I think I did well in keeping my definition short and sweet in light of the lengthy ones out there that say pretty much the same thing. If you agree, I'll print myself an award certificate using my Monica Geller software suite. Now, if we were to break this definition down to include even fewer words, I believe we could get by with "the influence of ideals." Ideals, of course, are principles or standards that we adopt based on what we believe is morally right. And these ideals influence every aspect of our lives. So, while politics is typically understood to be either *personal* or *governmental*, I think it's safe to say that it's all personal. After all, ideals are what we decide they are. And governments are made up of…well…us. And who are we? Let's find out.

We are all like sheep that have gone astray.

ISAIAH

We are inclined to do only evil all the time.

GENESIS

Our hearts are, above all, deceitful.

JEREMIAH

We fall short of God's glory.
ROMANS

We are incapable of doing good.
JOHN

Our works are unworthy of salvation.
EPHESIANS

These attributes describe the very nature of human beings. According to Scripture, none of us are even remotely good. And yet we often behave as if these apply to anyone but ourselves. Picture two bags of spoiled peanuts arguing back and forth over which bunch is more edible. Imagine that these same peanuts are also shouting at the ones laying loose in order to convince them which bag they need to be in. When it comes to politics, this is us in a nutshell. See what I did there? Be warned. The cringeworthy dad jokes do not end here.

If you've ever watched shows like *Meet the Press* that feature political commentary, you may recognize the term *polarization*. If you're not already familiar with this word, you might think it has something to do with glaciers or snow like I did. Polarization actually refers to the sharp opposition of one group toward another. Much like the Hatfields and McCoys, Capulets and Montagues, Jets and Sharks, or the Bloods and Crips, each polarized group staunchly defends its turf, whether that turf be geographical or ideological.

Many of today's political debates are reflections of these infamous rivalries. Instead of remaining civil, the back and forth between opposing politicians can get downright nasty. Gone are the days when my great uncle and my grandfather could lovingly tease each other about their opposing views and then depart with a hug. Here to stay are political smear campaigns whose ads sling dirt on men, women, and their families in the name of Christian values. Sadly, politicians aren't the only ones doing this.

Shortly before our most recent presidential election, I witnessed a heated argument on Facebook that erupted from a moderately civil political discussion between two outspoken Christians. The statement that lit the burner expressed amazement over how a person could call themselves a Christian and yet support a political party that favors the pro-choice position concerning abortion. Not only did this statement give away the party that this person was loyal to, it questioned the salvation of those who supported opposing political parties. And, as expected, others began to join in the fight. When the smoke finally cleared, all that remained was a mess of smoldering text that God's name was dragged through over and over.

But avoid foolish controversies, genealogies, dissensions, and quarrels about the law, for they are unprofitable and worthless.

TITUS 3:9

While arguing with each other over politics is indeed a fruitless activity, I do feel that it's worth our time to explore the many facets of this institution that cause us to grit our teeth and raise our defenses. According to this next verse from Jude, there are indeed things worth fighting for. Being a good contender, however, may require a withdrawal from skirmishes over worldly matters.

Beloved, while I was making every effort to write you about our common salvation, I felt the necessity to write to you appealing that you contend earnestly for the faith that was once for all time handed down to the saints.

JUDE 1:3

Another touchy issue we often disagree over is whether or not a Christian should drink alcohol. While the Bible does not condemn enjoying a beer or glass of wine, it does caution us about this risky activity due to its potential to stain our credibility as proclaimers of the gospel. This can occur when someone who is not well-versed in Scripture assumes that drinking alcohol in any capacity is a sin, and that Christians who drink it are being hypocritical. And so, while having a drink is not necessarily a wrong choice for us, being seen doing it can give Jesus a black eye and cause people to turn up their nose at the Christian faith. This teaching is found in the last few verses of the 14th chapter of Romans, where we are urged to either do these activities in private or make the best choice of not doing them at all. Decisions to ignore the Bible's instruction on this matter will not be treated lightly.

Whoever heeds instruction is on the path to life, but he who rejects reproof leads others astray.

PROVERBS 10:17

The verse from this teaching in Romans that we'll focus on for the remainder of this chapter teaches us that merely speaking out in favor of these questionable activities can get us into trouble. Of the many passages of Scripture we'll read together throughout this book, this one ranks pretty high on the ladder of importance.

So whatever you believe about these things keep between yourself and God. Blessed is the one who does not condemn himself by what he approves.

ROMANS 14:22

Years ago, as I was preparing to teach this very lesson from Romans during Sunday School, I began to consider similar activities that might lead others astray. Right off the bat, using foul language in public came to mind. But I was sure God wouldn't want us doing that in private either. It had to be something we publicly support that we should either remain quiet about or disassociate ourselves from altogether. That same evening, a political argument on TV caused a light bulb to appear over my head. As the tension was building between two representatives of opposing parties, I realized how hard it must be for an outspoken Republican to share the gospel with a Democrat and vice versa. These two weren't just disagreeing. They were downright nasty toward each other over a matter that was more trivial than controversial. I mean, who has a heated argument over which type of deodorant a person should use? That's not really what they were talking about, obviously. But I've slept since then. It was on that level of importance, though, I assure you.

Given the hostile nature of politics today, I am convinced that aligning ourselves with a political party is something Christians should either do in private or not do at all. Does this mean that people who are saved should not vote or become politicians? Absolutely not. Anyone who steps up to the plate with the achievement of God's will at the forefront of his or her campaign should have our support. One intent on running for office might simply weigh the importance of identifying with a party whose name will only add to the hatred that professing the name of Jesus will have already stirred up. Did I already tell you that people hate Christians? They do. This kind of hatred, however, is to be rejoiced over.

Blessed are you when people insult you and persecute you, and falsely say all kinds of evil against you because of Me. Rejoice and be glad, for your reward in heaven is great...

MATTHEW 5:11-12

As Christians, we are hated because of who God is. However unpleasant, this is pretty much unavoidable. The Bible assures us that this polarization between Him and humanity will always be a thing. More and more often, however, God is hated because of who *we* are. This occurs when we associate Him with things He's not associated with—things like politics. Instead of Christians, we're left-wing or right-wing Christians whose identities are associated with the polarized behaviors these labels carry. For the record, I do understand that a party can be mislabeled by people who claim to be its members and yet behave contradictory to that party's values. I get it. Christianity is in the same boat as I explained already. But political parties are not churches. And salvation isn't attributed to being a member of any of them.

Whenever you're engaged in a heated political debate, know that God is not in the ring with you, nor is He fighting alongside your opponent. There's no one political party that God considers good. How do we know this? It's because God's definition of 'good' is perfection. To Him, a thing cannot be called good if it is even 1% not good. And so, being that you and I are among the things that are not good, we can be confident that the institutions we create based on our human ways of thinking are equally flawed. Regarding abortion—a topic we'll dive into shortly—this issue does not represent the line between good and evil. A political party that opposes the practice is not more godly than the one who embraces it. As a result, no one is given clearance to cast the first stone, or any stone for that matter.

Do not judge, and you will not be judged. Do not condemn, and you will not be condemned. Forgive, and you will be forgiven.

LUKE 6:37

Another aspect of political culture is *Christian nationalism.* Like polarization, this appears to be an issue that was only given a name in recent years. Rather than pertaining to anything official, Christian nationalism is merely an idea that points to our country being favored by God due to its identity as a

"Christian nation." The reason I used *our country* instead of *a country* in my definition is that this is largely an American sentiment—a sentiment that people in other countries find rather amusing. To many of these, the United States of America is anything but a Christian nation. From afar, they see our movies, our entertainment, our glamorization of drugs and alcohol, and even how we manage to turn something as random as a hamburger commercial into something lewd and sexually suggestive. Not to mention the constant violence they see on the news—citizens waltzing into schools and churches with assault rifles and opening fire. To them, the USA is an incubator for the worst behavior our world has ever produced.

In the same way that I attribute my salvation solely to God, I believe that my placement in this world is according to His design. While I am grateful to have been born in the USA and am even moved by Bruce Springsteen's patriotic songs, I do not "bleed red, white, and blue," as they say. Rather, I see myself as living in a foreign land in which I do not monumentally belong. Because my home is not of this world, I've taken strides to keep from becoming too attached to it. I am a law-abiding citizen and am happy to tell anyone that I am an American, but I do so knowing that God gives no special nod to the people of the United States. To suggest otherwise would be to associate God with something He's not associated with—favoritism. Rather than loving us for who we are, God's love is *despite* who we are. And His love is worth disassociating ourselves from this world and from the many labels a fixation upon it can create for us.

> **But God demonstrates his own love for us in this: While we were still sinners, Christ died for us.**
>
> ROMANS 5:8

Returning to the topic of Christian politicians, the Pharisees might have served as the politicians of Jesus' day. And I wouldn't be surprised if the saying, "crooked as a politician," was coined for these guys. The term "hypocrite" certainly was. Used to describe an actor who played multiple roles and wore multiple costumes, Jesus was actually the first to use this word to point out someone being two-faced. And he directed it at the Pharisees as the disciples chanted, "Go Jesus! Go Jesus!" I may need to fact-check that last part.

Anyway, not only were the Pharisees staunch enforcers of their meticulous laws, they were also crafty with loopholes that allowed them to sneak their way around those laws. For example, to keep people from working on the sabbath, the Pharisees decided that a person could not walk more than a certain number of steps away from their home. Because one's home was designated according to where that person's belongings were, the Pharisees would strategically place items they owned along paths that allowed them to walk as far as they'd like on the sabbath. Should this matter be brought before a judge today, a verdict might involve arguments over the topic of our next chapter by lawyers who are equally crafty with loopholes. Criminal intent may be disproven in our earthly courts, but there'll be no pleas of innocence in the heavenly one.

For God will bring every deed into judgment, with every secret thing, whether good or evil.
ECCLESIASTES 12:14

Before we move on, let me point that the Bible's claim to be beneficial for teaching and training has been proven a million times over. This applies to correction as well. And I'll be the first to point out that being corrected is *not* fun. None of us want to learn that something we've been doing is wrong. When this happens, not only must we admit that we were at fault, we are faced with having to make changes. When it's the Bible that exposes our error, it can be a life-altering event that involves intense emotional distress. Historically, realizing God's truth has prompted people to leave their churches, end relationships, and even walk away from their jobs, all after having invested years of time and energy in them. This is God's discipline. And it's *all* good.

For the moment all discipline seems painful rather than pleasant, but later it yields the peaceful fruit of righteousness to those who have been trained by it.

HEBREWS 12:11

God disciplines those who He loves. He wants us to recognize our error so that we may redirect our paths toward Him. It may be hard to envision, but there's nothing negative about these experiences. That is, unless we resist.

Whoever knows the right thing to do and fails to do it, for him it is sin.

JAMES 4:17

If you're a very vocal political person who's made it a practice to shed a negative light on those you don't agree with, what new direction might God be leading you today? Are you so wrapped up in this behavior that the thought of ceasing it causes you distress? If so, this may be God telling you just how much He loves you. It may be His way of drawing you close to Him. Should additional topics we discuss expose His preferred path for your life, I pray that you will not be resistant to Him the way I once was.

Years after my initial awakening, I began to tell myself that there was nothing wrong with the way I was living. I must have done this twenty times over the course of a year before it dawned on me that no person had suggested otherwise. This suggestion was coming from God, to whom I had surrendered once before. But I hadn't surrendered completely. This is a requirement that all of us must meet in order to obey Jesus' command to love God with *all* of our heart, *all* of our soul, and with *all* of our mind. As God showed me, partial obedience is not obedience at all.

CHAPTER FOUR

RIGHTS & FREEDOMS

As American citizens, we all have rights. What is a *right* exactly? When it's not describing the opposite of wrong, a right is an entitlement provided by a higher authority. These entitlements allow us to *do* or *own* something. Some might even say that we have a right to *be* something. Because being is synonymous with doing, including this entitlement is certainly fitting. While it's important to know what a right is, it may be more beneficial to know what a right *isn't*.

Although there are many things we can do or own that no one will dispute, not all of them are considered rights. For example, I can pour myself a cup of coffee at any time of the day I wish. And I can crank up the volume of the Seinfeld reruns that I'll watch while enjoying my coffee. These things represent freedoms. Unlike rights, many of our freedoms have not been decreed by a higher authority. Not individually, anyway. A freedom becomes a right when it is protected by law and cannot be denied us. So, while my wife cannot take away my rights, she can certainly march in and turn the volume down on the TV. That's one of her freedoms—a freedom that I wouldn't mind being taken away.

So, you get the picture concerning rights. Right? Good. I could go a step further and point out that a right is not always right, but we'll establish that during the next chapter. So, where can we read about all these rights that we have? Our Constitution is a good place to start, but the list is by no means comprehensive. Some of the rights it declares have been reinterpreted to establish numerous other rights. This effort can also result in rights being taken away if they are found to infringe upon other rights. This is a painstaking and arduous process that involves people with amazing amounts of mental stamina.

Now, concerning the rights that have been declared for us, none of them are obligations. In other words, a right *to do* something must be coupled with an equal right *not to do* what that right enables. Otherwise, it may not be called a right. The things we must and must not do as citizens are according to our *laws* rather than our rights. Laws involve consequences, whereas rights do not. You'd think so anyway. Today, due to spikes of racial tension and political unrest within our country, citizens are deciding on their own whether our rights should have consequences.

One morning at church, I listened as a member of my small group asked for some advice about voting.

The inquirer was a woman in her fifties who felt that none of the presidential candidates touted values that matched her own. In response, one of the more politically-minded members of the group told her that she needed to vote no matter what. Regarding her indecision, she was advised to simply vote for the lesser evil. Another person affirmed this advice by quoting the following Bible verse to demonstrate our obligation to vote.

Jesus said to them, "Render to Caesar the things that are Caesar's and to God the things that are God's."

MARK 12:17

This was Jesus' reply when he was approached by Pharisees who asked him asked whether or not people should pay taxes. Between their motives of not wanting to pay taxes and wanting to catch Jesus declaring something heretical, both may have applied. In his response, Jesus explained to them that, because Caesar was of a higher authority and had made paying taxes a law, doing so was an act of obedience. Voting, however, is not an obligation. Therefore, it is not associated with obedience or disobedience. Vote, don't vote…it's purely up to you. The American government will not single you out and persecute you if you choose not to vote. The American people, however, will.

If you've ever told someone that you didn't vote, you may have been called anti-American or told that you no longer have a voice of influence over our country's leadership. This shaming of nonvoters has led many people to feature their "I voted" stickers in the images of their Facebook profiles. While many who've done this are proud to have voted, others have confessed that they were only trying to eliminate themselves as potential targets for the politically hostile attitudes among their Facebook friends. The Supreme Court does not hear cases involving this type of persecution by citizens, of course. But it did put an end to nonvoter persecution by state governments.

In 2018, state election commissions began to deregister residents who had not voted during two or more primary elections. When this matter was brought before the Supreme Court, the verdict declared that there can be no consequences for not voting—even if the penalty was as little as having to pick up a pencil and reregister. This was corrected by requiring notices to be sent to inactive voters, asking for confirmation that their name and address have not changed. Instead of being purged for choosing not to vote, only a failure to respond to these notices may result in deregistration. So, instead of feeling obligated to vote for a lesser evil, a choice not to vote for *any* evil should sit well with you.

Voting is about casting our good names, which are associated with Jesus' name, in the direction that our hearts lead us. At no time should we raise our hands in favor of things that do not align with our moral convictions. Not liking meatloaf and being asked to vote for light or dark gravy on top may be a different story, though, especially since you don't have to eat it. Just revolt and head toward the salad bar.

Yet another right that has been attacked as of late is *free speech*. Following the murder of black citizen George Floyd by white Minneapolis police officer Derek Chauvin in May of 2020, a behavior known as *cancel culture* began to emerge. It started as outrage among citizens prompted organizations to declare public statements of solidarity that expressed their condemnation of racism in America. In response, the American people took to public forums and began attacking these organizations for having solidarity statements that did not appear genuinely empathetic. And then they turned on each other.

Today, we watch as our fellow citizens continue these attacks that mimic the Pharisees' angry demands for the crucifixion of Jesus. These witch hunts involve years of tweets, images, and text from social media channels being sifted through daily and often stripped of their context in order to label public figures as racists. In response to the demands that their victims' jobs and dignity be placed on the chopping block, organizations that employ them seemed to give in without a fight, lest they too become targets of public scorn.

If you've witnessed this activity, you may recognize that this racism police force, for the most part, is not orchestrated by black men and women. Instead, its work is carried out by those who see themselves as heroes whose goodwill gestures deserve praise from the black community. In their minds, these deeds grant them free passes from becoming a target themselves. Instead of good Samaritans, however, this cancel culture has produced a breed of individuals who lurk in the darkness just waiting for an opportunity to pounce. You probably recognize this behavior from the Bible. If you can't pinpoint whose it is, here's a hint. It's not Jesus.

Your enemy the devil prowls around like a roaring lion looking for someone to devour.

1 PETER 5:8

One area within the US Constitution that fuses rights and freedom together concerns our ability to worship. Often referred to as our *right to religious freedom*, this very first amendment reflects the order of priority given to the church. In it, the government is prohibited from interfering with religion. So, does this make worship a right or a freedom? If we read carefully, I believe we can discern that our worship is a *freedom* that Congress has no *right* to take away.

AMENDMENT I

Congress shall make no law respecting an establishment of religion, or prohibiting the free exercise thereof...

Contrary to popular understanding, the purpose behind what is called the *separation of church and state* places equal importance upon religion. When it was introduced, this notion merely pointed out the vital societal roles of each institution. The church's role was to build spiritual leaders, while the government was responsible for congressional and industrial leadership. And both were seen as operating harmoniously beneath the sovereignty of God. However admirable, this message that Thomas Jefferson included in a letter to the Danbury Baptists Association of Connecticut in 1802 was nothing more than a mission statement. While the content of this letter is still highly regarded today, its modern interpretation may cause you to question whether people are reading the same letter.

Today, the separation of church and state is widely understood to be a mandate designed to protect the government from the threat of Christian influences.

Those who insist on this version may be missing that Mr. Jefferson was a church member, as were each of the founding fathers who people struggle to identify and yet insist were not. Many of the men and women we recognize for their impactful leadership roles outside the church were equally active inside. And so, instead of labeling the church as a potential enemy of the state, it should be obvious that our third president was merely reiterating the high value that both he and our first amendment placed upon the church. It *should* be. The fact that leaders within our government openly share the alternate version strongly suggests otherwise. There's also evidence that people simply *want* Jefferson's letter to say what it doesn't say. If we can do this with the Bible, a dead President may be seen as fair game to use as a means to retroactively denounce American Christianity.

Much like the organizations we talked about earlier who caved under the duress of the people, many state officials have given in to the demands of citizens who claimed that the presence of inscriptions of the ten commandments on public property is unconstitutional. When this matter landed on the docket of the Supreme Court in 2005, however, its ruling stated that having God's laws visible in public areas did not pose a conflict with the Constitution, whose every decree was directly influenced by the Bible. In other words, declaring that the ten commandments do not belong would be like saying that wieners have no place inside a hot dog.

I present this not to give you ammo to fire back at people who display hostile attitudes toward Christians. Rather, my goal is to expose various tactics that prompt us to do things we don't have to do and keep us from doing what we are entitled to do. If you've ever been told not to impose your Christian beliefs on others, you've experienced this first-hand. In fact, the person who gave you this command was doing the same thing. By telling you what you should not do based on their perception of right and wrong, that individual was imposing his or her beliefs upon you. Feel free to fire away with this one. Just be gentle when you do it.

Each time we encounter our oppressors, we must treat them as if their names were recorded in the book of life at the same time ours were. Just as the Apostle Paul was called away from a life of harming Jesus' followers, these people may very well have their day with the Lord at a later date. Everyone we meet is a potential brother or sister in Christ worthy of being the target of our prayers. Why be selective over who should experience God's goodness within us? When we pray for the families of those who were beheaded for their faith, should we not also pray for the executioners? When we pray for missing children, should we not also pray for their captors? When we pray for our President, should we not also pray for his opponents? Jesus, who prayed for his own opponents, captors, and executioners, assures us that we should indeed.

Love your enemies, do good to those who hate you, bless those who curse you, pray for those who abuse you.

LUKE 6: 27-28

CHAPTER FIVE

ABORTION

A few weeks after completing the manuscript for this book, the Supreme Court overturned the Roe vs. Wade court decision of 1973 that made abortion legal. This was the result of a decision to reexamine whether the US Constitution supports abortion as a right of the American people. While I regard this ruling as a good thing, the fact that this decision was not reached years ago just kind of dulls any desire I have to celebrate. After all, our Constitution hasn't changed. In case you're wondering whether this chapter is still needed, let me point out that division over abortion has only escalated since this ruling. It's also worth noting the ban on this practice was not a collective effort by our government to get right with God. Just as the Bible was excluded from the decision to allow abortion, it does not appear to have been taken into account here. And so, I do not share the belief that this was a "win" for Christians. If anything, we are hated even more because of it.

Before this decision, the laws protecting abortion were highly varied among the states. Looking back, it's clear that the motive behind the limits beyond which an abortion may not take place is one of suffering. Another factor was *viability,* which refers to the point at which an unborn child may survive outside the mother's womb. Because no two children are the same, the point at which a child is deemed viable was left to be determined by medical professionals based on data from the countless number of premature births that have occurred within our country.

Of our 50 states, 13 had disregarded a baby's suffering and allowed viability to become the chief factor in their laws that contended for abortion. In other words, these states allowed abortions all the way up to the point that a baby could be born and survive. As for the accuracy of doctors' viability calculations, those must have all been spot-on. During my research, I found no legal disputes by aborted babies, and no malpractice suits by patients claiming that their baby suffered undue harm during a procedure. These measures assure us that none of our abortion laws factored in human *value*, which is God's sole criterion.

Before writing this chapter, I read how authors who choose to tackle this subject should refrain from using words like *baby* and *child* as they unfairly lead audiences to become emotionally stirred. Because I've never seen a birth announcement that included the word *fetus*, I opted to ignore this advice. The nature of an unborn child is not dependent upon whether a pregnancy is wanted or unwanted. Claiming otherwise is clearly an effort to lead audiences to become emotionally numb. And the last thing I want to do is downplay the value of a human being.

Another topic that often comes into play during discussions about abortion is capital punishment. Over the years, I have watched several Christians mocked on TV for being in favor of capital punishment and yet against abortion. Upon being called hypocrites by their interviewers, their inability to explain why there was no conflict between the two caused them to be humiliated. Should this be a concern of yours, I'm here to help. For me, the easiest way to discern between abortion and capital punishment is knowing that one is murder, and the other is punishment for committing murder. The book of Genesis clarifies this for us.

Whoever sheds human blood, by humans shall their blood be shed; for in the image of God has God made mankind.

GENESIS 9:6

We see this same teaching again in the book of Numbers.

Do not pollute the land where you are. Bloodshed pollutes the land, and atonement

cannot be made for the land on which blood has been shed, except by the blood of the one who shed it.

NUMBERS 35:33

According to Scripture, the reason we're not to commit murder is that each of us was created in God's own image. This may seem trivial to you and me, but it's a huge deal to God. An unspeakable amount of love went into the design of every single human being. To Him, we are worth every drop of blood Jesus shed on our behalf. We are not to harm each other, steal from each other, gossip about each other, lie to each other, call each other names, or harbor ill feelings toward each other. He doesn't want us to even *look* at each other with wicked thoughts in our heads. When we do these things, our actions are aimed at God because we belong to Him. You and I are His precious belongings, and every breath we take is sacred. Of all the beautiful sentences in the Bible that convey God's adoration for us, I can think of none that were as lovingly written as this one.

Before I formed you in the womb I knew you, before you were born I set you apart...

JEREMIAH 1:5

These words that God spoke to Jeremiah inform us of

His love as well as His plan for our lives—a plan He made before we took up space inside our mothers' womb. We also learn that the act of conception is by God's own hand. Because His love for us existed before we did, there can be no point in life, born or unborn, that we should deem ourselves or others disposable. We simply are not ours to dispose of.

Do you not know that your body is a temple of the Holy Spirit who is in you, whom you have from God, and that you are not your own? For you have been bought with a price.

1 CORINTHIANS 6:19-20

When it comes to arguments in favor of abortion, a common defense stresses that a woman has a "right to her own body." You'll see this written on many of the handmade picketing signs that are carried during pro-choice rallies. This, of course, is a basic human right that also applies to men. Our physical bodies are indeed our own to make choices for. What makes this argument invalid in its support of abortion is the word *own*. From conception to birth, at no time is a baby part of the mother's own body. In fact, a completely separate genetic structure can be realized within just a few short weeks of conception. While a baby relies upon its tether to a mother's womb via the umbilical cord during pregnancy, the unborn child's life, health, and vital signs are not measured according to the mother's health. This assures us that a baby is an entirely separate human being. It also exposes the Supreme Court's recent decision as merely an extension of our existing laws that prohibit the murder of *any* human being.

So, what about rape? Shouldn't rape be grounds for abortion? This is a question that no man, woman, or government institution should be made to answer. If your concern is over the anguish one might experience having a child serve as a reminder of a horrible act of violence, I would question why one should feel that killing a baby would put an end to this anguish. An abortion would only pile guilt upon an already suffering heart. Fear of this guilt often accompanies one's unwillingness to give a child up for adoption in favor of abortion. In these cases, the idea of one's child being alive and apart from the parents becomes equally unbearable. And so, killing the child is seen as a means of wiping our emotional slates clean. But this isn't what occurs. Regardless of our status as believers or nonbelievers, we all experience guilt. And there's only one way for our hearts to become free of it.

During my college years, I became acquainted with a young lady who would eventually have an abortion. She was the love interest of a close friend that I grew up with. During their dating relationship, my friend informed me that she had become pregnant, and neither of them was happy about it. While the couple's next steps were not made public, the fact that she never appeared pregnant spelled out that she had either miscarried or had an abortion. About fifteen years later, my friend informed me during a heart-to-heart conversation which of the two had occurred. Neither were Christians. And yet both suffered what was described to me as the worst bout of depression imaginable.

Despite having complete confidence in their decision to abort, the couple became traumatized soon after being informed that the procedure was a success. Unfortunately, their relationship did not survive the pain each suffered, and the girlfriend wasn't around anymore. But I did have an encounter with this lady some years later. And during our brief conversation, she decided to open up to me. After describing much of what my friend had told me, she added that no effort she made eased the terrible feeling of guilt over her decision. She explained that she could not understand why she felt so utterly horrible. No one had shamed her, including her parents. And yet, she considered suicide as an option to escape her emotional distress. Just as I was about to ask about her faith, she lit up and exclaimed that it was only through coming to know Jesus that she had been freed of this burden she carried. On that day, her smile was brighter than I had ever remembered.

Regarding our insistence that abortion still be available, instead of making concessions for why we should be able to circumvent God's will, we should do everything within our power to *accomplish* His will. This calls for the surrender of our desires that conflict with His. Because you and I are imperfect beings, we can be certain that *all* of our desires will pose a conflict. As humans, our ability to reason has always been subject to the things we see, hear, taste, touch, and smell in this world. God, however, is not *of* this world. He's also perfect in every sense. So it goes without saying that He sees things very differently than we do.

"For My thoughts are not your thoughts, nor are your ways My ways," declares the Lord.

ISAIAH 55:8

If you're a Christian who supports abortion but would never undergo such a procedure yourself, know that this attitude does not create a safe zone. If anything, it's even more dangerous than being a full-blown advocate. Adding to the persuasion that the murder of a precious life is a right thing to do can never be right, especially when your moral convictions tell you it's wrong. We are not to condone sin for others, nor are we to even partially support the things God detests. We are to proclaim the truth rather than our varied perceptions of it. And when our pride stands in the way, we are to lay it at Jesus' feet as an act of repentance from our natural tendencies to be at odds with God's will and with each other.

God's wants His grace to be detected in all we do, especially by those who oppose us. Regarding abortion, we must understand that calling someone who does not believe a fetus is a human being a murderer is the wrong approach. The overturning of Roe vs. Wade may have fanned the flames, but it's only increased our opportunities to show love to our neighbors who feel jilted by it. For those who see this court ruling as an opening to reevaluate the laws associated with our next topic, I would proceed with caution. The potential fallout of such an event might warrant a new name for our country…

The *States of America.*

CHAPTER SIX

GUNS

According to the US Centers for Disease Control and Prevention, 39,707 of the deaths that occurred in the United States during 2019 were caused by guns. Of these, 23,941 were attributed to suicide, while acts of homicide claimed 14,414 lives. The remaining 1,352 were either accidental deaths, military casualties, or those whose nature was not determined to fall within these categories. These stats are in addition to what must be a staggering number of injuries resulting in disfigurements and permanent disabilities. As these numbers appear to hold steady year after year, one has to wonder whether our country has opened a door that was never meant to be opened.

As a life-long resident of Tennessee, I have witnessed the widespread celebration of gun ownership. Here, it's not uncommon to see the regard for our Constitution's 2nd Amendment and the Holy Bible as equally sacred. In fact, if you're not fluent in the art of street fighting, you might want to avoid adding your opinion against guns to even the friendliest of conversations. As for me, equipped with my son's PlayStation controller, I've fired them all over the years; some equipped with lasers for taking out Storm Troopers. While I've never felt led to own an actual gun, I find the most compelling reason for having one is that they're pretty cool. Conversely, my least compelling reason for owning a gun is all too often the number one reason others have—the need for protection.

If you were to approach someone whose bumper sticker or t-shirt touts the 2nd Amendment, you might ask them to share their thoughts on the correlation between it and gun ownership. Depending on where you are in the world, having a white flag handy when you attempt this may be advisable. Jokes aside, because people love to discuss things they're passionate about, you could very well end up with a new friend and a free cup of coffee. Experiences will vary, of course. But you can count on being informed how this portion of our Constitution ensured the states' ability to form a *militia*—an army of regular citizens—to help protect their freedom.

Because militias were not issued weapons the way our armed forces are today, the states were dependent upon residents who had their own guns. Today, with united states who are no longer fending for themselves, and with multiple branches of trained soldiers at the ready in nearly every one of them, the understanding that this amendment guarantees citizens the right to own firearms is somehow undisputed. As additional amendments, such as the

14th prohibiting illegal search and seizure, were taken into account over the years, the 2nd began to take on a new meaning among the American people. Instead of helping to protect our government, guns became a necessary means of protecting citizens *from* the government—a sentiment that the United States Constitution does not recognize.

With mass shootings occurring on a near-daily basis in America, protection from each other has equally become a motive to own a gun. Employees at Subway gunned down by a customer who didn't want mayonnaise and the murder of a college student by his roommate who became disgruntled over the noise of popcorn chewing are among recent headlines that would seem unimaginable when I was growing up. And yet, news of this nature is commonplace within our children's lives today. As much as I'd like to point out that our government is not adding fuel to this fire, I just can't do it.

One afternoon, while shopping for groceries, I overheard a man on his cell phone urging the person on the other end to prepare for government agents to arrive at our homes and force American citizens into some kind of submission. And being prepared, according to this man, included "buying lots of bullets." Having roots in southern culture, I've learned to detect facetious rhetoric, however unsettling its content. So, after supposing that this man wasn't completely serious, I dismissed his words as mere crazy talk. Several days later, I encountered this same banter on TV. This time, the crazy talk belonged to a Congresswoman whose political party opposes our President and whose pleas for the American people to ready their guns were met with shouts of "Amen!" If you were listening from the next room, you might have sworn that a church service was on TV. Given the topic of this speech, some who were watching may also have felt it was church.

The longer I watched this event, the more shocked I became. As if the speech wasn't concerning enough, its delivery from behind a podium with an official government seal was downright disturbing. I couldn't believe it was being allowed. This woman was stirring up the crowd in the same manner the ring leader of a lynch mob might have done ages ago. According to her, factions within our government were planning to go door to door and inject micro-tracking devices into our bodies against our will. While our government does encourage people to protect themselves from the pandemic that our world is experiencing, this story was pure hogwash. In Tennessee, we use words like *hogwash* to describe things that are obviously untrue. Strangely enough, the bogus nature of the Congresswoman's story did not seem obvious to her.

As she raged on, I supposed there must be some very frightened people out there. If betrayal and endangerment on a massive scale isn't scary enough, these tracking devices are often understood to be the antichrist's method of administering the mark of the beast—more hogwash. But hey, if your motive is to scare the public into becoming armed to the teeth, I guess you can do a lot worse than telling people Satan is in the Oval Office. Still, despite the lies and slander, the most unfortunate aspect is that this woman identifies as a Christian. To be fair, coupling this type of rhetoric with Jesus will get a lot of people asking where you go to church. But not because they want to visit.

...when you grow old, you will stretch out your hands and someone else will gird you, and bring you where you do not wish to go.

JOHN 21:18

In case you're unfamiliar with this passage from the book of John, these words from Jesus were directed at Peter to inform him of the reality that would await his decision to devote his life to sharing the gospel. So, how does this relate to guns? It doesn't really at all. But it's one of several verses I found during my research that political extremists have used to motivate people to turn their homes into an armory. And it's a prime example of how God's Word can be stretched and twisted to suit one's equally twisted agenda. So, are our lives truly in danger? Do we really need to be ready to shoot our public servants? This is essentially what the enraged Congresswoman and many others would have us to believe. Why? Ahh, now *that* is the question. I'm surprised none of you asked it before now. Why is it so important that we believe these lies? This question has a simple answer, but I've chosen to complicate it by dedicating the next chapter to examining these motives.

So, did I find any real evidence to support the possibility of our nation's government going rogue? None. Not only is there no record of our country's leaders unlawfully forcing its citizens to act against their will, there are numerous measures in place within the framework of our government to prevent such a thing from ever happening. But I don't need these facts to become convinced. I already know this will never happen. And I know that assaulting government officials with a deadly weapon under the suspicion that it *can* happen is punishable in a court of law. And so, while our government has allowed citizens to own guns, the Supreme Court rejected the idea that doing so gave the American people the right to take up arms against government corruption (United States v. Cruikshank, 92 U.S. 542, 1875).

Now that we've nailed this down, we can begin our Bible lesson.

Servants, be subject to your masters with all respect, not only to the good and gentle but also to the unjust.

1 PETER 2:18

Here's another verse that I found to be particularly relevant.

YOU SHALL NOT SPEAK EVIL OF A RULER OF YOUR PEOPLE.

ACTS 23:5

Just like you and I do, God often sends His texts in all caps to let us know He means business. While the idea of being servants to our government can leave a bad taste in our mouths, His Word pairs servitude with our obedience to individuals and institutions alike who assume roles of authority over us. Our obedience and respect toward our government are reflections of our respect and obedience to Him that he wants others to witness. Just as our laws contain no clauses that support our holding an officer who oversteps the law at gunpoint, God does not give us any leeway in His expectation that we resist our urges to fight fire with fire. This can be extremely hard to do when anger and our desire for fairness come into play. But then, Jesus was never at the mercy of these emotions. Thus, it is God's will that we not be either.

So, what if an officer comes into our home, ties us up, and begins beating us? Are we just supposed to sit back and do nothing? This is an extreme example that none of us should be building up our defenses over. Even so, the Bible is clear there are no safe passages from being mistreated, lied to, mocked, and abused by others. As Jesus pointed out to Peter, these things come with the territory of being a Christian. I do, however, feel strongly that God's will for our lives is not that we cower in the face of danger. We're not doormats for others to trample on. At the same time, our reactions toward those who treat us like one serve as opportunities to radiate the amazing love God has for us as well as our oppressors. Resisting our desires to harm those we feel threatened by may never seem natural to us. But then, turning away from our nature as humans is what repentance is all about.

You have heard that it was said, 'Eye for eye, and tooth for tooth.' But I tell you, do not resist an evil person. If anyone slaps you on the right cheek, turn to them the other cheek also.

MATTHEW 5:38-39

I hope you've understood by now that this chapter isn't really about gun *ownership*. To be honest, I don't think you'll find a verse in the entire Bible that tells us we shouldn't have one. There is, however, a wealth of Scripture that may challenge the *motives* behind our choices to own a gun. Here's just one of the many verses in the Bible that address what may be among the most common motives behind the number of gun-related deaths that I presented at the beginning of this chapter.

Do not be afraid; do not be discouraged, for the LORD your God will be with you wherever you go.

JOSHUA 1:9

Today, our news is saturated with stories meant to spark fear and hopelessness in us. Based on our behavior, I'd say the schemes are working. These two reactions, however, are meant to be overcome. Just as we are commanded to avoid being controlled by our anger, rising above fear and hopelessness is an absolute. And we can achieve this by trusting in God who has authority over us and by letting our obedience to Him overshadow our tendencies to take matters into our own hands. Lastly, our motive for doing these things must be our love for God in light of who He is and all He has done for us. That's it. Trust and obey. If you're wondering whether there's another way, consulting a church hymnal will lay your query to rest.

CHAPTER SEVEN

DECEPTION

Back in 1955, French astrologer Nostradamus gained worldwide notoriety after publishing a collection of predictions about the future that actually came true. Well, people think they did anyway. In reality, his predictions were so creatively vague that there is little agreement upon which events he may have been describing. Because his little puzzles could be put together in any number of configurations, each of Nostradamus' predictions seemed to come true over and over again. Whenever a new event matched one that was pegged previously, his puzzle was reworked. This, of course, exposes Nostradamus as a phony prognosticator. But that didn't stop people from believing he was the real deal.

While Nostradamus' work was fairly harmless, his fans share a common bond with followers of today's conspiracy theories—the belief in falsehood. What sets conspiracy theories apart is their portrayal of individuals, organizations, or entire governing bodies as being involved in evil schemes that the theorists themselves may not fully believe. What's important is that readers believe. The more followers the theorist gains, the more intense his sense of power over people's minds becomes. And, little by little, the theorist is transformed into the evil Dr. Doofenshmirtz.

So, how does a conspiracy theory work? Good question! Each theory is essentially a story or statement about something "secretive" that may either currently be happening or may have happened already. There are conspiracies about the future too, but a good theorist will not risk his influence not panning out. To make the story believable, the theorist intertwines facts and fabrications to create a scenario that has the *potential* to raise suspicion. As theories go, a well-crafted one cannot outright be proven false without some effort—an effort that a strategically chosen audience isn't likely to make. By definition, a theory cannot be true either. Instead, its very existence relies upon a cloudy gray area.

If you've ever watched the movies *Pelican Brief* and *Conspiracy Theory*, both starring Julia Roberts, you saw how theories about government coverups turned out to be true. You may also have noticed that these two are essentially the same movie. Though Julia's roles are reversed, each one features a conspiracy writer on the run from corrupt individuals whose dastardly deeds were exposed by one of the writer's theories. Much like any trade, there appears to be an art to conspiracy theorizing that involves a hyper-awareness of current events, a knack for reading audiences, and a master's degree in B.S. Let's look at some actual conspiracy theories that have caused a stir in recent years.

Closed Walmart shopping centers are secretly being used by the government to stockpile weapons in preparation to declare martial law.

Cloud-like condensation trails behind passenger jets are seeding the atmosphere with cyanide in order to gradually reduce the overcrowded American population.

The COVID-19 pandemic began intentionally to test software designed to identify people by scanning only the area of the face above protective masks in preparation for the binding and gagging of citizens by the American government.

Yoda is actually Miss Piggy.

Ok, that last one is mine. But it's true! They have the exact same voice. We are being deceived, people!! While this is kind of how it's done, you likely saw right through all four of those bogus statements. That's because I left out the most important element of a conspiracy theory—influence. The people behind these wild ideas do not just copy and paste them onto Facebook. You'll read them there eventually, but only after they've been passed around and reported on by conspiracy-minded journalists. A conspiracy theorist targets special interest groups who are already engaged in paranoid political discussions. Posing as an ally, the theorist informs the audience members that they are being deceived and deserve to know the truth. And the "truth," of course, is just more lies. For those of you who are into history, there's a book out there that has the first conspiracy theory ever crafted. It's called Genesis.

The serpent said to the woman, "You surely will not die! For God knows that in the day you eat from it your eyes will be opened, and you will be like God, knowing good and evil."

GENESIS 3:4-5

If you're at all familiar with the QAnon movement in our world today, you may recognize it as mirroring Nostradamus' puzzle party. It started when an anonymous individual known only as 'Q' gained quite the following after sharing vague tidbits of "secret government information" online. Because these little clues were designed to shed a negative light on the American government, Q was believed to be an informant in the White House who was exposing corruption among our country's political leaders. This led followers to forge all sorts of warped conspiracies that, in their mind, gave Q credibility— credibility that was lost after Q began making predictions about the future that didn't pan out. At this, some bailed. Others just rearranged the puzzle.

As I mentioned earlier, effective conspiracy theories are at least *somewhat* believable. What baffles me is the totally unbelievable nature of claims that this Q was insinuating. I mean, this stuff was WAY out in left field. And yet, Americans by the droves, including many who identify as Christians, were eating it up. For the life of me, I still can't wrap my head around how anyone could believe that well-known politicians were gathering in a secret chamber beneath a popular pizza place in Washington DC to sacrifice and then eat human babies. I mean, surely the pizza wasn't *that* bad! Yes, I'll be here all week. I know it sounds insane, but this is indeed one of the more popular beliefs shared among those influenced by QAnon, whose ring leader Q has since been exposed as a young computer hacker with no connection to Washington whatsoever.

During an interview with several individuals who separated from the QAnon movement, one man confessed that a history of following conspiracy theories had sparked so much hatred in him that he was unwilling to think rationally. He explained how he wanted the lies to be true so badly that he lost touch with reality and even destroyed relationships with family members who tried to reason with him. His may sound like an extreme case, but there are followers who refuse to believe that Q was a fraud and are still waiting for their leader to resurface.

Now more than ever, conspiracy theories and the Bible are closely associated. They're not *related*, mind you—not even remotely. But where one is, you'll likely find the other. Instead of the Bible putting crazy ideas in people's heads, people with crazy ideas are picking apart Scripture to find verses they can mold into something that affirms their suspicions. While this is essentially conspiracy theorizing in reverse, the motive is the same. So, what do people gain by doing this? Along with the power trip we spoke of earlier, there's fame and fortune to be had by anyone who can convince the world that God has endorsed their delusions.

If you were to browse Amazon for books about the end times, you'd find a great number of titles about government conspiracies, secret cults, and encrypted messages, all with references from the Bible as their roadmap. Instead of reporting what they learn, authors who produce this type of content are on a mission. Rather than glorifying God, their goal is to glorify themselves for having put words in God's mouth that He never spoke and for uncovering mysteries of the Bible that never existed.

In vain do they worship me, teaching as doctrines the commandments of men.

MATTHEW 15:9

Today, there are more books about 666 than there are pages in the Bible. In the book of Revelation, we're told that this number is somehow tied to the antichrist's identity. What many people fail to realize is that this man's identity is already fully fleshed out for us. His attributes, however, are scattered among 26 chapters in the Bible—some in the Old Testament, some in the New. And the verse that tells us about the number 666 is not one of them. Yet so many people base their entire conclusions on this verse alone. If they can somehow tie this number to a public figure they feel is evil, they can proclaim to the world that an innocent man is the object of God's wrath. While there is indeed a challenge coupled with 666 in the Bible, the popular understanding of its purpose is way off base. How do I know this? Because everyone who's taken this approach has consistently ignored this next verse.

But know this first of all, that no prophecy of Scripture is a matter of one's own interpretation.

2 PETER 1:20

Because the topics of these biblical exposés are by no means limited to the end times, one might wonder how best to recognize the false teachers who author them. For those who share this concern, there are two characteristics to look for that give them away.

The first is evidence that the author has no interest in embracing Scripture as a whole. You may equally detect this among prophecy-centered evangelists and individuals who testify to having received new revelations from God on YouTube. While there are many passages in the Bible that speak against those who do this, I believe these hit the nail right on the head.

Behold, I am against those who have prophesied false dreams," declares the Lord, "and related them and led My people astray by their falsehoods and reckless boasting; yet I did not send them or command them, nor do they furnish this people the slightest benefit," declares the Lord.

For you will no longer remember the oracle of the Lord, because every man's own word will become the oracle, and you have perverted the words of the living God, the Lord of hosts, our God.

JEREMIAH 23:32, 36

The second characteristic of false teachers is much easier to spot. They're not selling Jesus. While you and I associate false teachers with erroneous claims about the Bible, these bearers of lies may come from all angles. Some are selling fear, others hatred. Regardless of the message, false teachers all prey upon ignorance and weakness. Today, as lies and deception become increasingly overwhelming in our world, we must be able to distinguish them from the truth. Just as hope and hopelessness cannot live together within the same heart, one cannot be the bearer of truth while under the influence of lies.

See to it that no one takes you captive through philosophy and empty deception, according to the tradition of men...rather than according to Christ.

COLOSSIANS 2:8

Dear children, do not let anyone lead you astray.

1 JOHN 3:7

Discouraging as it may be, evil and hatred are not going anywhere. With no hope for achieving a counter culture of truth, love, and forgiveness on a worldwide scale, it is our responsibility to foster this environment in our homes, in our churches, and in our relationships with each other as we carry the good news of our risen Savior into the world. Hang in there, friends. Our big exit from this earth is coming. When, you ask? Well, that's a tough question. I mean, people have been arguing about that for ages. I'm just not sure I can address it without writing whole new chapter. Ok, fine. I'll write it, but only because you asked.

CHAPTER EIGHT

RAPTURE

For every issue that lies beyond the walls of our churches, there's another that sparks dissension among God's people from within. For instance, a change in the style of music or the order of events within a worship service can stir up sour attitudes toward the pastor or minister of music. Services that stretch beyond the scheduled closing time can be equally off-putting to members of the congregation who want to get a jump on the Sunday afternoon crowd at Cracker Barrel. I see the grins out there. I too have spontaneously smelled fried shrimp during the closing prayer.

When it comes to doctrinal divisions within the church, nothing fans the fire quite like the rapture. What is *the rapture* exactly? It's an event that God has promised will take place on a day in the future. On this day, members of God's church, which consists of everyone who has ever placed their trust in Jesus, living or dead, will experience a bodily transformation and ascend toward the sky to be in the presence of our Savior. The Bible teaches us that this event will serve as our rescue from the terrible times that follow, which are reserved for those who will not have made a decision to trust in Jesus. We're also told that the rapture will occur within a period of seven years, whose timeline is framed by specific events that are named in Scripture.

For the most part, the endless disputes among church members are not over what will happen during the rapture. We're pretty much in agreement on that front. It's the *when* that gets everybody all in a frenzy. Indeed, many slices of toast have been hurled through the air during discussions over when the rapture will occur. But why? How can God's Word command us to be united and then send us to opposite sides of a boxing ring? It doesn't. But this is happening anyway. I'll explain why shortly. First, let's take a look at what the Bible has to say about all this. Jesus is up first with evacuation instructions for a frightening event that he says will occur sometime in the future.

Therefore when you see the abomination of desolation which was spoken of through Daniel the prophet, standing in the holy place—let the reader understand—then those who are in Judea must flee to the mountains.

For those days will be such a time of tribulation as has not occurred since the beginning of the creation which God created until now, and never will again.

MARK 13:14, 19

Regarding this "abomination of desolation," it appears to mark the beginning of some very tough times that lie ahead. As Jesus pointed out, these tough times will not have occurred before the abomination shows up. He also told us that Daniel had something to say about this event, so let's look at his book next.

And there will be a time of distress such as never occurred since there was a nation until that time; and at that time your people, everyone who is found written in the book, will be rescued.

DANIEL 12:1

In this verse, not only do we recognize the text that Jesus was quoting, but also words that describe the rapture—the rescue of God's people from this terrible distress that lies ahead. Coupled with the two verses from Mark that we just read together, this text informs us that the abomination of desolation is tied to the beginning of the great distress *and* the rapture. Both events will occur "at that time." So, when does "that time" fall within the seven years? Let's find out.

From the time that the regular sacrifice is abolished and the abomination of desolation is set up, there will be 1,290 days.

DANIEL 12:11

As we study the book of Daniel, we learn that this abomination is the antichrist who will enter the temple in Israel and cause the sacrificial worship to cease. The temple becomes desolate when the people inside run for their lives toward the mountains. This very teaching is mirrored in other verses as well. The words in this particular verse are spoken by an angel in response to Daniel's questions about these seven years. And the angel's reply informs us that 1,290 days (three and a half years) will follow this event. While the abomination is given a specific day within this timeline, the rapture is said to occur "at that time," or within a proximity close enough to be associated with the abomination. And so, while I am convinced that these four verses settle all disputes over when the rapture will occur, I do urge each of you to study their corresponding chapters for yourselves.

Now that the Bible has nailed down the timing of the rapture for us, let's dive in and see what all the fussing is about. First, let me point out that the word *rapture* does not appear in the Bible. It comes from the Greek word *rapio,* whose meaning "to be caught up" was ideal for the Latin translation of this verse.

After that, we who are still alive and are left will be caught up together with them in the

clouds to meet the Lord in the air. And so we will be with the Lord forever.

1 THESSALONIANS 4:17

In English, rapture means "to snatch." So you can see why it was not used in modern translations. It just doesn't have the same meaning. And yet this is the name we've chosen to use. Personally, I don't like the word. But then, nobody thought to ask me if I did before it was assigned to this event. If they had, I would have insisted that we stick to what the Bible calls it.

And do not grieve the Holy Spirit of God, by whom you were sealed for the day of redemption.

EPHESIANS 4:30

See what I mean? Like the event itself, there's beauty and grace in the word *redemption*, whereas rapture belongs in the title of a horror movie. I guess eliminating a syllable was important. Anyway, the decision to use this word hasn't caused any major train wrecks that I know of. So I'll back off, but only because I'm fixing to drop the hammer on another one of these renaming blunders. That's right, *tribulation period*. You're next!

To be fair, this infamous seven-year stint doesn't really have a name attached to it. In the Hebrew context, this period is referred to in the Bible as a *week*. And that wasn't gonna fly. So, at some point in history, it was deemed appropriate to refer to it according to the activity it's associated with— *tribulation*, which means "great trouble" according to the dictionary. Unlike rapture, this word is actually used in the Bible. So we're good, right? Not so fast. There's a reason why Oreos were not named "Chocolate Wafers."

As we just learned together, our big exit via the rapture will occur just as the trouble begins. And we also determined that only half of this seven-year period is in trouble. So, when we splattered the entire seven years with the name "tribulation period," it created a paradox. What was once understood to be *before the trouble* has morphed into the "pre-tribulation" idea that the rapture will occur just before these seven years commence. This has equally impacted those who believe the Bible describes a "mid-tribulation" rapture, as they must now clarify whether they mean *in the middle of the period* or *in the midst of the trouble*. Any way you slice it, we now have competing views, each side insisting that the other's interpretation of the Bible is wrong. The heartache behind this is knowing that arguments exist between two parties who don't realize that they actually agree with each other. Indeed, *pre-trib* and *mid-trib* can mean the same thing.

While those who support a "post-tribulation" rapture were unaffected by this, their approach was poorly thought out from the beginning. If both Christians and non-believers were to endure the entire seven years, God's promise to rescue us would be null and void, as would the central message of the Christian faith. Unlike the pre-trib and mid-trib positions, teaching this one would be very dangerous indeed.

I appeal to you, brothers, to watch out for those who cause divisions and create obstacles contrary to the doctrine that you have been taught; avoid them. For such persons do not serve our Lord Christ, but their own appetites, and by smooth talk and flattery they deceive the hearts of the naive.

ROMANS 16:17-18

To sum up, the Bible teaches us that the rapture will occur toward the middle of the seven years to rescue the church from the great trouble that God will impose on those who declined Jesus' invitation to trust in him. If you've been following along in your Bible, you observed that this truth is written plainly in black and red. While our understanding of when the rapture will occur is rather trivial in terms of our salvation, churches often place great importance upon declaring their position on the rapture's occurrence within their doctrines to demonstrate their interpretation of Scripture. Although this is a necessary practice, it can indeed result in division among churches and church members who share a common understanding.

If you're thinking I may be making this problem out to be bigger than it actually is, consider whether a label like pre-tribulation or mid-tribulation played a part in your choosing a new church to attend. Did you read into various doctrines, or was seeing a church's position on the rapture enough for you to eliminate it as an option? If only the *potential* for this kind of misunderstanding exists, it's a big problem. Unfortunately, it's not a *new* problem. The fallout has been ongoing for ages. As much as I feel driven to find solutions to the problems I detect in life, I doubt there would be much interest among churches in adopting a *pre-trouble mid-seven-year day of redemption* position concerning the rapture or even just backing out of the name game altogether.

As this train shows no sign of stopping, I take comfort in knowing that, in heaven, we will live and worship harmoniously alongside many who once understood the Bible differently than we did. Denominations will no longer be a thing, and none of us will be caught sneaking over to Jesus to ask how on-point we were with our interpretations. Instead, all our differences will melt away in favor of our common bond of victory and undivided love for our Savior. Wouldn't it be awesome if we could live this way now? According to Jesus, we're supposed to be already.

CHAPTER NINE

SEXUALITY

Over the last seventy years, our world has seen dramatic advancements in technology. Many of us who love movies and music have seen record players, 8-tracks, Walkmans, compact discs, VCRs, and DVD players become obsolete. We've also witnessed an enormous shift in the way we regard and react to sexuality. What was once an appreciation for being complimented with the words pretty and handsome has become a ruthless desire to be hot and sexy. In addition to pointing out the cancel culture we talked about earlier, the Bible identifies this behavior among others that will be prominent among people at the time of the end.

There will be terrible times in the last days. People will be lovers of themselves, lovers of money, boastful, proud, abusive, disobedient to their parents, ungrateful, unholy, without love, unforgiving, slanderous, without self-control, brutal, not lovers of the good, treacherous, rash, conceited, lovers of pleasure rather than lovers of God...

2 TIMOTHY 3:1-4

These descriptives conclude with an imperative for followers of Jesus.

Have nothing to do with such people.

2 TIMOTHY 3:5

As the sharing of barely clothed selfie images over social media becomes commonplace, many of us have become numb to the sexualization of our people. While attitudes toward this topic vary wildly among Christians, unbridled sexuality is not something that causes tension between us the way other topics we've discussed tend to do. Rather, this tension, called enmity in the Bible, is between us and God.

And I will put enmity between you and the woman, and between your seed and her seed...

GENESIS 3:15

The other day, I left the radio on after dropping my teenage daughter at school. As a musician, I enjoy all kinds of music. Even so, I rarely turn on the radio myself these days. Whenever I'm in the mood to transform my steering wheel into a drum set, I usually listen to songs from my music collection on my phone. Anyway, the song that was playing was one that I'd heard before, but not in a setting where I could make out the lyrics. I either heard it playing in another room or amidst the clanging of pots and pans while cooking dinner. Now alone with this song in the car, I began to hear blank spaces where there should have been lyrics. This, of course, was an effort to mask words that might land a radio station in hot water should they be heard over public airways. As these muted segments became more numerous, my attention was finally drawn to the lyrics. And what I heard was gut-wrenchingly vile.

Instead of turning the radio off, I chose to keep listening in hopes that the DJ might name who was singing it. I wanted to know whether this female artist was among those my daughter had mentioned in our conversations about our favorite singers. When the artist was not named, I figured the DJ must have done so before the song began because he did announce who was singing the next song. This was a name that you could know even if you never listened to the radio—a female singer who had been around for years and whose life was constantly talked about on TV. She might have even been in a movie. Her song was familiar as well. Now that my radar was on full alert, I listened intently to the lyrics, which I realized were being sung over a separate track with the singer's moans of sexual pleasure. As for her primary vocal, you'd think she ran a mile just before getting behind the microphone. This sultry and breathy singing style has been popular among female artists for decades. But it's come a long way since Marylin Monroe's "Happy Birthday Mr. President."

Within a seven-minute drive from my daughter's school to my house, I had been exposed to the audio equivalent of hardcore pornography. The "clean versions" of these two songs described masturbation, oral sex, and a fetish for being bound by a sexual partner—acts that no amount of muted swear words can cover up. No amount of muted swear words could have covered this up. Sickened by this, I wondered how often I had heard songs like these and just not paid attention. How often had my daughter? While I've never been the kind of parent who would nix access to public radio as entertainment for my two teens, I now am faced with whether my hard stance against visual pornography creates a conflict. Would I dare allow porn videos on my TV even if my wife and kids were doing other things and not paying attention to it? Would I hang a pornographic poster inside a closet that none of us really use? The fact that these two songs were ranked highly on the Billboard charts makes these arguments invalid. Our young people are indeed paying attention.

There is no fear of God before their eyes.
ROMANS 3:18

So, why have things become so sexualized in our country? The verse above from Romans pretty much spells this out for us. Money is also a factor. Simply put, sex sells, especially when our young people are the ones buying. Unfortunately, they're also what's being sold. Indeed, there's a form of sex trafficking in America that's perfectly legal. It's called Hollywood. Since we've already made an example of today's popular music, taking a look at the artists who pump out these songs seems like the natural next step. So let's go there for a bit.

Today, Paul Simon and Smokey Robinson would have a tough time getting a record deal as new artists. Both were attractive fellows, but they emerged during a time when sex appeal took a backseat to great music. And these two actually sold albums—millions in fact. While you can still buy digital music albums today, many fans are content to watch music videos online that you don't have to pay for. Paul and Smokey made videos too, of course. Seeing theirs, however, made you want their albums, whereas today's music videos lure fans to want the artists. This applies to pop as well as country music whose performers' marketability is often decided according to the potential number of fans who'll want to have sex with them.

If you feel I'm off base, just do a quick Google search about the demands of potential artists upon being offered a recording contract. Young men are asked to remove their wedding rings, and young women are asked to remove even more. The bigger the splash these artists can make with their bodies, the more money their managers and handlers stand to make. Music is still a part of all this, but it's quite common that a new artist has no involvement in the selection of songs they will sing if their voices are factored in at all. If you're a success, you might become the next Cardi B — a highly sexualized icon and performer of pornographic rap songs who our country celebrates as a role model for young American girls.

Being a Hollywood star, however, isn't always required to receive such notoriety. Thanks to social media platforms like YouTube and TikTok, a young person can make a splash as an influencer whose encouragement to follow one's dreams involves embracing homosexuality and gender neutrality. In addition to male and female, today's job applications allow applicants to identify themselves as *transgender* or *nonbinary*, thus trading their physical identity with one that matches their sexual desires. To these, being addressed with the pronouns "he" and "she" may be seen as offensive if they conflict with one's sexual identity. Some individuals even insist on being addressed as "they" to accommodate their lack of a streamlined attraction to one gender.

In light of all this, some have speculated whether God had begun to make mistakes over the last 70 years, putting females inside male bodies and vice versa. This behavior, however, is by no means a new phenomenon. It's been around since the days of Noah. Even so, I wonder what my grandmother would have to say about these sexual identities if she were alive today. I wonder what she'd have to say about marriages between two women. And I wonder what she'd have to say about TV commercials featuring open-mouth kissing between two men. But I guess it's not important. What's important is what the Bible has to say.

God gave them over to degrading passions; for women exchanged the natural function for that which is unnatural, and in the same way also the men abandoned the natural function of the woman and burned in their desire toward one another, men with men committing indecent acts and receiving in their own persons the due penalty of their error.

Although they know the ordinance of God, that those who practice such things are worthy of death, they not only do the same, but also give hearty approval to those who practice them.

ROMANS 1:26-27, 32

At the beginning of this chapter, we read together the Bible's instruction for us to have "nothing to do" with those who bear these identities. I'm confident that these words are not directing us to exclude, ostracize, or avoid any of them. These are God's children. They are our neighbors who we are to love as we love ourselves. A close friend who I've known since I was a teenager is now married to another man. Yet I seize every opportunity to throw my arms around him whenever we meet. I love this man. And there's truly nothing that I wouldn't do for him. My identity, however, is not *intertwined* with his as a Christian homosexual. Wait a sec! He's a Christian??? How is this possible? This is between him and God. But I suspect that his choosing to embrace that which the Bible speaks against is not unlike our own behavior.

Instead of inserting my own creativity here, I'm just gonna go with one of Jesus' examples. As his disciples, our houses are built upon solid rock. And it is our mission to lovingly influence our neighbors whose homes have foundations made of sand. This contrast between security and danger has never been more clearly presented. And yet our behavior is strong evidence that we've begun to believe the sand is the way to go. Maybe our neighbors will like us more if we can come up with a mixture of rock *and* sand. So we shovel in some political hostility, some relaxed feelings toward sexual behavior, and maybe toss in some bitterness toward others who aren't as "correct" as we are. As we become increasingly convinced that God is ok with our new hybrid foundation, we begin to add more and more sand to the mix. It might seem sturdy to us, but our violation of God's building code puts us in great danger.

There is a way which seems right to a man,
But its end is the way of death.

PROVERBS 14:12

For no man can lay a foundation other than the one which is laid, which is Jesus Christ.

1 CORINTHIANS 3:11

As the world becomes increasingly accepting of unbridled sexuality, we as members of God's church have equally become lax in this regard. Evidence of this is a common understanding among Christians that, if it's not intercourse, it's ok for unmarried couples. But is it *really* ok? All of it? Something tells me that it isn't. And that something is the Bible. While the lines we draw in the sand tend to shift with the tides, God's line between morality and immorality hasn't moved. Our condoning of sin to even the smallest extent is a very serious matter that God does not take lightly.

As parents, we don't want to be seen as old-fashioned prudes whose convictions have not progressed with the times. And so, we give a little here and a little there without ever considering why this negative stereotype exists. Have you ever thought about that?

I hope you will now. Don't worry about arriving at different conclusions because there's only one—we are being influenced by the world. Dare we entertain the idea that God is influencing this behavior? Is He driving us to allow our children to dress inappropriately? Does God want us to ease up on the content in movies that we allow them to see? Do His expectations regarding sexual activity give us some wiggle room to decide on our own what is acceptable? If God isn't initiating these things, why else would we be doing them? You see it now, don't you? Brothers and sisters in Christ, be extremely careful where you draw your line. In case you're wondering, here's where God has drawn His concerning every issue we've explored together and many more that we haven't.

All that is in the world, the lust of the flesh and the lust of the eyes and the boastful pride of life, is not from the Father, but from the world.

1 JOHN 2:16

Do not be conformed to this world, but be transformed by the renewing of your mind, so that you may prove what the will of God is, that which is good and acceptable and perfect.

ROMANS 12:2

One last thing. As a proud father, I love to show off my two children to friends and family members who either have not met them or haven't seen them in years. When I've been out and about with my daughter, I cannot count the number of times the compliments she received included, "You should be a model." In all her seventeen years, not once did these gestures of encouragement figure her for a Sunday school teacher, a missionary, or a caregiver to the elderly. Instead of pairing her potential with acts of service that would separate her from the world, she was informed of how she might best become like the world. And she was told this by as many church members as non-church members. You may disagree with me, but when it comes to encouraging our children, I believe we have a responsibility to aim a little higher. That is all.

CHAPTER TEN

CLOSING

Well, we've made it to the end of another lengthy study together. Unless I missed something, there were no earth-shattering altercations or disputes among you to report. No angry emails calling me out for presenting offensive material either. You guys were actually pretty quiet this time around. This is a relief. Sometimes you just don't know what to expect. Thankfully, this is not the case with God's Word. Instead of keeping us in the dark, the guesswork concerning our future has been eliminated.

In the Bible, the end is written for followers of Jesus. And it's pretty clear that global warming will not have not made humanity extinct. Vaccines will not have not depopulated the world, no American public figure will have become the antichrist, and citizens will not be controlled by secret government software. Bill Gates, you're off the hook! Unfortunately, the fear of things like this will still be rampant. And, given all we've learned together, it might be a stretch to say that only non-Christians will have these fears.

Let me remind us all that God is in complete control of this world. Let's not live our lives as though He isn't. As proclaimers of Christ, you and I who house God's Holy Spirit serve as the glue that is holding this world together. Though chaos exists around us, we are the band-aids covering the many self-inflicted wounds that humanity has created. God can fulfill this role without our help, of course. But He invites us participate in the achievement of His will on earth. Not only are we to work harmoniously with Him, but also with each other. Another absolute.

Live in harmony with one another.

ROMANS 12:16

During his time on earth, Jesus stressed how vitally important it is that we be undivided. The things he commanded us to do with and for one another include serving, praying, forgiving, encouraging, ministering, and even crying. Sometimes, instead of grasping for words to assure a grieving brother or sister in Christ that things will be ok, our tears may be the greatest expression of love and support we can offer.

And let us consider how to stir up one another to love and good works, not neglecting to meet together, as is the habit of some, but encouraging one another, and all the more as you see the Day drawing near.

HEBREWS 10:24-25

Misery isn't the only emotion that loves company, though. Joy loves it just as much. As you just read, being undivided means more than simply being in sync with one another's ways of thinking. The fulfillment of God's will for our lives requires us to actually be together. I know, I know. I creep up to the window to see if I can avoid whoever's ringing my doorbell too. And I'd just as soon text someone rather than call them or, God forbid, show up at their door so they can also pretend not to be home. It's so odd how we've gotten to be this way despite the need God placed within us to be in the physical presence of others. While you and I are united as members of the *global* church, our brothers and sisters in Christ who live in Zimbabwe have needs that only a *local* church can fulfill. By the way, if you actually live in Zimbabwe and are reading this book, let me know and I'll create a special edition with an alternate far-away country. Canada maybe.

Anyway, I'm not gonna drag this chapter out. It's not even a real chapter. Just kind of a back-end introduction, which is appropriate since I didn't add one to the front end. But it gives me the opportunity to tie together all we've learned. With that said, if you take nothing else away from our time together, know that, as humans, our sole purpose on this earth is to bring glory to God. We can do this individually, but we were created to to do this collectively with a shared focus upon Jesus Christ. As long as we remain at odds with one another and harbor bitterness within our hearts, we'll be hard-pressed to achieve this. Simply put, united, we stand. Divided, we fall. Undivided, we do both, but we can lift each other up and bear one another's burdens as we await our arrival on a new earth where we will finally love one another the way Jesus loves us. Finally.

❖　❖　❖

Dear Lord, we have fallen far. In going our own way, we have become numb to the wickedness and perversion that surrounds us. The images of You we bear are uniquely skewed according to the degree our hearts have been influenced by this world. We call evil good. We hate one another. We slander authority. We pass judgment. We lust. We deceive. And we've no appetite for Your Word. We are divided.

Lord, there is no written word fitting to describe the extent to which we are rotten. How is it that You allow us to speak Your name at all? How??? How can Your Spirit continue to dwell in such rancid temples? How??? How can our lives be worthy of even the tiniest dot of Jesus' blood? How??? LORD, HAVE MERCY ON US!!!!! We have lost our way.

We have done a great injustice by ostracizing those who You desire for Your own. We have twisted Your

Word to suit our selfish desires. We have robbed You of the glory that is due You. And our gratitude for all that You have done for us is grossly insufficient. Falling on our faces does not bring us low enough to be in Your presence. And yet we come before You according to Your instruction and ask that You intercede on our behalf.

Father, forgive us for what we have become. Do not put away your shears, but continue to prune the dead branches we sprout. Clear our paths that are overgrown with the sin we embrace. Move our hearts to desire humility instead of righteous glory. Create a thirst within us for Your Word that far exceeds our desires for the things of the world. May the ugliness we have placed upon You fall on us instead. Gather Your lost sheep, Lord. Cleanse our hearts and bring us back to You.

In the wonderful and powerful name of Jesus Christ, I pray.

Amen.

www.ingramcontent.com/pod-product-compliance
Lightning Source LLC
Chambersburg PA
CBHW030026290326
41934CB00005B/505